21st Century Coastal American Verses

Poems by

Zack Dye

Zack Dye's work
can also be found in:

Shout! An Anthology of Resistance Poetry & Short Fiction
"The Tides of Macon"

21st Century Coastal American Verses

Poems by

Zack Dye

Copyright © 2020 by Zack Dye

All rights reserved.

Published in the United States by
Not a Pipe Publishing
www.NotAPipePublishing.com

Hardcover Edition

ISBN-13: 978-1-948120-73-9

Cover Art and Design by Benjamin Gorman

DEDICATED TO

Mary Pearl Mikkelson, Roberta Graham,
Victoria Aceves, Beuhlah Jackson,
Jane Snyder and Angela Casale

Contents

Forward 1
opening doors 11
Making Sense 12
Infinity 15
   So Often I don't Pay Attention to Even the Most Obvious Things 17
One eye up, Captain 20
Saturday Night Flick 21
Stethoscope 23
If I had the patience of a billion years 26
Today 27
30 28
Cemetery 30
Tiny Chapters 31
The First Six Days In Hamilton, NY 34
Daughter to the Spinning Pulsar 41
Mammals 44
Un Muerte in El Cajon 45
The Wolves are Out 49
The Atlantic Was Born Today 51
The Albino Mexican 55
Monday 61
Agapanthus 62
Those Neverending Math Equations 65
Another Giant Wave of Sadness 67
The Freezin' Scene 72
The Brain of Gravity 77
Leashes 81
Dog Park Haikus 82
What Would You Broadcast into the Universe? ... 83

Tight Spaces 85
Hunger 86
Agapanthus II 87
Independence, Oregon 88
Order 90
Galactic Novenas 91
A Day of Haikus 93
Ice Cream in the Freezer 96

FORWARD

As a Mestizex lawyer in New York City, I learned early on how important a haircut is in the boroughs. If I went to any one of my neighborhood barber shops in Bushwick or Ridgewood, they would cut my shit close and make it look real tight, and for the next two weeks, a lot of my conversations on the streets would start with, "*Qué lo que?*" or "*Qué tú hace?*" Speaking Mexican Spanish taught to me by my grandmother, my fluency ingrained by summers in Mexico and formal Spanish elementary school in San Diego, I didn't really know what those phrases meant at first. But you learn. Language is really just a variety of constructions based on "survival." That really means that if I wanted to maximize my privilege and get through the bodega quicker or get an extra helping of fried *plátanos*, I worked with the new code words I was offered. Besides, Dominicans are some of the best people. They drink Presidente, they make better *mofongo* than their Puerto Rican neighbors, they like *béisbol*, their women are very kind, and every Dominican has rhythm... whether they actually do or not.

Still, when you spend your day in a law office, you realize the partners and associates don't think much of you when your hair is that short. They think you're there to do anything but practice law even if you have a tie on. So you're careful about how long your hair is. Instead, you let the old ladies at the salon with *tijeras* cut it because everyone knows the dudes at the barber shop *no saben usar tijeras para nada*.

The layers of contextualized racism are deep in America, and especially in New York. One of my favorite stories from my time in New York that embodies the fluidity of race is when I did Steve Black's taxes. That wasn't Steve's last name per his birth certificate, but Steve was Black, like almost literally Black. So that's what he had us call him. I did sort of a street tax thing. I didn't work for H&R Block anymore; I made my money practicing corporate law. For some extra cash and to help out those that needed some extra "knowledge" I would do some people's taxes every season. My preferred clientele were people who were likely to get "robbed" by a regular tax preparer services *and* Uncle Sam. One night, sometime in May, I'm at the spot on Amsterdam just south of Columbia University having dirty, dirty, dirty $4 happy hour martinis with two cute, young, Jewish women who were new to the city. Steve comes over and gives me $100 bucks in cash and says, "Yo, there you go my Nig. I gotchu. Thanks for hooking it up."

"No worries, I'm glad they got that to you."

"Yup, yup, all good dude. We hooking it up now." Looking at our friend J.J., the bartender and pointing down at me, Steve said, "Hey, I got Z... I'm gettin' Z's next drink."

One of the Jewish girls looks at me and says, "I thought you were a lawyer."

"I am."

"So what was that? You're a dealer? You get him drugs?"

"Get him drugs?!"

"Yeah, that cash? He was paying you back for drugs or something, right?"

I cackled and cackled and cackled some more. "I did his taxes," I say, "and he just got his refund. But I don't charge until my folks get their money back." She hid sheepishly, putting her martini to her face drinking very little - mostly just hiding from the embarrassment of her racism. To be fair, it was an unfamiliar scene for her, and the layers of potential American prejudice are thick and hard to wade through.

My name is Isaac Joaquín Dye. I'm named after my Mexican great-grandfather. But everyone calls me Zack. When you grow up where half your family are white people with a predilection for racial epithets, Zack is more palatable. "Eeesssak," as they struggle to pronounce it, is not a perpetual fight you want to have. Especially when you're just a kid. It's not fair. It's just one of the many moments to which you adapt where people of lighter skinned mixed ethnicities find it easier to make ourselves as white as possible rather than trying to really even feel comfortable with our real names. So my folks, intentionally or not, just killed the "I" and moved on with "Zack". This even persists systematically on some level today. I have asked the State Bar of Connecticut and New York for almost 15 years to put the accent over the "í" in my middle name. Still, all my mail comes back with just that little, piddly dot over the "i".

When I was nine, all the kids at Mexican summer school in Guadalajara made fun of me because I spoke funny Spanish. They called me Gringo all summer and never let me forget I was an American. For a few days, I came home crying, until my dad finally said, "This is how it is. You're never gonna be Mexican here. And you'll never really be white in America. Sure, we look white, and we'll sound white and people will want to think we're white. But we're not white. Our people are brown. And really, *our* people are all the people that don't get to be white. So, you gotta stop crying about it. It's not fun, and you won't really feel like you ever belong anywhere, but as long as you do the right thing and help the people that need help, they'll let you belong with them."

America is a very scary place to not be white. People get uncomfortable very easily, and it worsens the darker your complexion is. If I spend too much time outside in the summer, everyone at work will inevitably notice. To make themselves feel safer, they say, "Oh, wow, you sure got outside this weekend and got a nice tan." The truth is that I can get pretty brown, like Mexican brown, beaner brown... the kind of brown that makes white people uncomfortable, so they prefer to think that I'm just tan rather than not-white. This doesn't really make me feel any better or worse about my heritage, but it makes me feel safe. It is another reminder that no matter where I am, I'm safer being white, and I have the luxury of making that choice. At the office, I'm more trusted if I'm white. On the streets, if an old lady doesn't know me, she feels better if I'm white. If a police officer sees me, I'm safer looking white, and I certainly don't speak to the officer casually or with A.-A.V.E. like I might when I'm more in my element, comfortable with friends at some bar.

When I don't feel a need to be a white lawyer, where I'm within a variety of other people who don't care what I do for a living (and in fact, probably have little desire to remember I'm a lawyer throwing back more whiskey than I should), I'm happy to talk like everyone else talks in parts of Brooklyn or spots in Oakland, without pretense, like we do at home with our families, black or brown. So my pattern of speech can change from trying to have a Mexican or Dominican accent in Spanish to using slang or very clear diction in English. White American society wants people a certain way, even though they won't admit it to themselves. They certainly don't want them black or brown. Even the most progressive minds can suffer these prejudices. Like, for example, Hunter Thompson's Polynesian lawyer in Fear and Loathing in Las Vegas. The real attorney in that story is a hero of mine: The Brown Buffalo, the Chicano lawyer working in the Fruitvale district of Oakland, Oscar Zeta Acosta. But in America, authors and publishers knew that while a Mexican lawyer isn't absurd, it's an unpalatable truth that ruins absurdity and scares even the fans of Gonzo Journalism. No, American readers prefer their lawyers white and not accepting receiptless cash for guerilla income tax returns which help poor minorities get everything to which they're entitled. History tells us that is *not* the Hamiltonian nor Jeffersonian American Dream. Americans would rather hear crisp and deferential diction, without inflection, accent or commonality. Just like the American constitution, white America always wants things a certain way - their way - like presents under a Christmas Tree, or fireworks on Independence Day, or a Three-Fifths Compromise.

But things have never felt right in that "certain" way for me. I've been gifted with immense talents and physical attributes that make it easier for me to take advantage of those gifts. If you're really brown or black, you know there's no bootstraps to pull up, there's not enough extra credit to do, there isn't just hard work - you know the deck is stacked. When you spend enough time in criminal court or migrant housing, you know there're no aces in those decks. There aren't even face cards! My successes are built on the literal backs of so many others who never had the opportunities America is willing to give me just because of my carefully manicured hair style and skin color. So, from where I stand, if you can climb a few rungs on the ladder, then it's your job to throw down a rope. We're in this together, all of us. You don't get to take your ball and go home. You get to share your ball... and ultimately that's the real gift.

So for my adopted Mexican sister who had a tough run of it from the first day on Earth, to my nephew who is learning now that America doesn't want you unless it can use you, and the whiter you are the better, and for my Abuela who knew that being brown was a curse in America, so she spent her days with light foundation to make her look as white as she could, I know this is a very ruthless country that will do whatever it can to take any shortcoming and use it against a person. I am challenged to understand how to help all my black and brown siblings when America doesn't want me to be brown - they want to help silence minority voices and to silence minority advocacy. As James Alan McPherson writes in one of the stories of his Prize Winning <u>Elbow Room</u>:

> *"...he still thought I was accusing him or calling him to account.*
> *He said, 'People *do* grow. You may not think much of *me*, but my children will be great!'*
> *I said , 'They will be black and blind or passing for white and self-blinded. Those are the only choices.'"*

I hope that, regardless of the color of anyone, my experience and the experience of so many others continues to foster crystal clear vision for our children. But I understand that by "passing for white" I live in a certain sense of "self-blindness."

From ivy walls of my East Coast private schools to lecture halls of my law schools, from recalcitrant arrestee to zealous advocate of the arrested, from interpreter of laws to speaker of the many American dialects, white America wants me self-blinded so that I willingly aspire to be just like those founding fathers: privileged; ignorant of those people they hijacked, beat and murdered. They want me complicit in their rape of their own souls; they want a co-conspirator to take the fall with them.

From within such frames these poems are meant to challenge minds that think race and language belong to specific borders on the spectrum of skin color. Our collective American racism identifies everything we do, no more extricable from our bodies than the alcohol that shreds a cirrhotic liver. Because we're all really the same in body and mind. We are all equally capable. We all deserve the same opportunities. Anything that works against that thought is cruel. More specifically, it's wrong.

Baldwin wrote so many great books but I am most fond of *Giovanni's Room* because it speaks to the construction of the self that I have spent a lifetime understanding, rebuilding and improving:

> "For I am—or I was—one of those people who pride themselves on their willpower, on their ability to make a decision and carry it through. This virtue, like most virtues, is ambiguity itself. People who believe that they are strong-willed and the masters of their destiny can only continue to believe this by becoming specialists in self-deception. Their decisions are not really decisions at all—a real decision makes one humble, one knows that it is at the mercy of more things than can be named—but elaborate systems of evasion, of illusion, designed to make themselves and the world appear to be what they and the world are not."

It is this mastery of deception that has molded me. Even though white society has rewarded me by deceiving parts of myself from others, I am aware of these rewards and their unfairness. And, in choosing some behaviors over others, I am humbled by what I feel I should hide. When you realize that you are not allowed to be yourself and that you are, outside of dark bars and your own well-lit man-cave of a basement, a fraud trying desperately to survive a cruel and racist world, you are humbled. You know that you owe a debt to those that are unable to deceive the masters of this cruel world, caught in the sights of nasty men believing nasty, selfish things. Some of us get the "good fortune" to realize that before our deathbeds we must reckon with how we got the benefits to which we originally felt we were entitled. But no one is owed nothing, nor should they be. We must confront those privileges we've been afforded and the unhappiness felt by so many others because like Hayden says as he finishes *Middle Passage*, all of this America was and is actually a *"Voyage through death... to life upon these shores."* Someone else has died a violent and unjust death for me to exist today.

So, this book seeks to mine through the deathly voyages that so many were forced to make. Or the voyages of death which found life upon these shores only to quickly rape, murder and rename it all. I am embarrassed that I deceive so that I may enjoy the benefits of those murderous or enslaved voyagers; that I occasionally luxuriate in the privileges of safety I'm allowed, if I am hidden and complicit. I rage on the inside that I cannot do more, that even when I yell, America's murderous soul is likely deaf to my anger.

Instead in my "free" time, I quietly canvass, or teach or write. These are the poems of that rage and confusion, where I am forced to reckon with the prejudices of something as stupid as a haircut, because to cut it just right is a key to vaults of wealth but to cut it even a touch shorter than that is to face the glares of suspicion thinking that I might be there to steal what *they* have already stolen.

-Isaac Joaquín "Zack" Dye

Oakland, CA
September 16, 2020

OPENING DOORS

The man
Paces briskly back and forth
Between the coffee shop and the pharmacy
Anxiously anticipating the exiting patrons
He takes three steps
From the left to the right
Looking through the window panes
Holding the door; waiting on anyone
Politely asking all of them for change.

October 18, 2009
Brooklyn, NY

MAKING SENSE

That sound, it drips so slowly down my chin.
The notes of crisp refreshment fall off
The flesh like juice from the very same fruit.
Such pristine freshness... and it dangles,
It holds,
Steady over the skin
Upon the fat, above the flesh and outside the circulation;
Falling, as it should, to the ground.

Drip,
Drip,
Drip
Like that venom within the snake's bite,
In the digestive saliva of the fly,
In the paralyzing spider bite.
Those sounds empty to the ground.

The spiraling sensation of the nature
As it rings inside the vision
Trees standing shadow
Attending a brilliant quickening
The sunshine pouring
Into the veins of plants and animals
Alike they share the power,
Alike they share the sound

And the fury,
The angry side of man,
Attacking the vessels of his own livelihood;

The bark spread across barren land,
The upset view of a vista felled
A man's own ideal deserted in his own blow -
The ax leveling the playing field,
Cliches for the tolling bell of time.

What is that fine scent?
That delectable flavor flowing from tongue and nostril -
Sensational little orifices exulting in powerful symbols,
The ringing percussion of a parade gone mad,
Roses and fresh popcorn,
Bubblegum and queens,
Marshalls and hot dogs,
Success and victory.

Or defeat...is that the ashen muck
Festering in the depths of the olfactory,
Where the angry stench of God's combustion burns
The cells to their malignant conclusion,
Where that sad state of death is
The embers smoldering to char,
Where the carbon is so useless
That the organism loses any value?

Of course, to inhale the scene is to taste,
To quench the thirst of the most fruity inkling -
The luscious peach surrounding the pit -
The protein inside the cherry;
A reason
To nurture and to love, to hold, to care,
To raise in the image,
To living, to lead, to love.

Still, the feeling is so fleeting so often.
It tastes like the bitter pill

From the daily morning regimen,
The people's own lubricant and the earth's own oils -
Potions from the back of the cart.
In the laudanums of such sensual release;
Tasting a falsehood that is so sallow,
An emptiness; venturing into the taste of nothingness.

So I feel: what questions can we ask in the absence of sense?
That potential energy is reduced to kinetic exhaustion -
The conflicting impulse of all energy.
Is what we tactically grasp is the inevitability of irony?
In the regression of infinite math equations;
At the end of a zillionth calculation
That pie might reach infinity...
That is something I can feel?... Thinking I can touch uncertainty

When I grasp for a lack of understanding
I understand what you feel... what I feel -
Generically the same feeling - that we build to an end to build again.
Where everything at rest is at the precipice of motion;
This continues forever?
Who understands that feeling!?!
That we do not understand our feelings,
Maybe that is what I feel.

January 24, 2008
Brooklyn, NY

INFINITY

So rarely will she dance.
Still she screams that she dances
...over...
and over again
...she screams
she yelps at the injustice,
she hollers at the in humanity

so often does she explain that which I don't know.
so often she illuminates the obvious
and the light shining from behind her
only illuminates my misunderstanding

she so often misunderstands
what, she is want to know
what, so lucky am I to know
which is not my job

that she misunderstands at all is the child
in the bough
in the break
in the beauty of beauty

that perfection is comprehends is imperfections
that the words are so forced from the books that explain
truth
and still
even my majestic lady cannot interpret truth from
untruth

that imperfection comprises her at all
that she knows

in the beckoning evening
and the discomfort of uncertainty
she stands for herself

as she stands for me, and for us all.
that the perfections presumed to the everyman are the
fallacies of beauty
the fallacies of heaven
the mistakes of people

she breathes softly in the morning
and her breast heaves beneath
my hand touches her cheek
my soul reaches for her spirit
searching in the fog of evening
disappearing in a perfect mist
in the midst of imperfection
my miracle that still she rested next to me
in the heaving mistakes of the midnight slumber
such dreams of my mine lost in the dreams
that she dreams
that I might witness perfections of imperfection.

January 30, 2008
Brooklyn, NY

So Often I Don't Pay Attention to Even the Most Obvious Things

are we holding each other
yet?
this overwhelming overt tenderness;
an awkwardness
an awkward -
of strange hitherfrom... hitherto?
the words they make so little sense
but I have said that before.
so, what makes sense?

stay here please
you always make enough sense
in those readings,
in those meanings.
even in your absence
love makes no sense;
the strange composites
equal to more than
the sum of the parts.
the everythings of touch,
the caress
the love...

such entangled intangibles
the couches
the glances
the sexy dresses
the everything...

of everything
i want the everything

such that was wanted;
in the middle
the beauty of our own love.
and still that means nothing.

for example:
that sweet woman.
the sweet sensation.
the debates I engage in;
the loves that I horde.
the sensational.
the her;
a skinny, leggy beast.
(lovely loveable beast):
"The Sprawled Out Exhaustion of Ecstasy"

the words of the monster
that the beast beached
upon the shore is all
the beast wanted
that you stand
all before me
like the cars passing
in the night
intermittently the drunken fast food
memories of Heinrich Heine's Allee.
kann ich gut machen?

remember all that mattered
(mattered so little except to you
all that felt)...
felt so much to everyone.
the conundrums of the everyman

there is no argument

she was so beautiful
as she dances into and out
of the night dreams -
she was undeniably there;
her undeniability
i am still exhausted as such
is her fortune
is her richness.

the lavish tarnishing,
a life framed perfect,
she dances,
dancing so far away
that this matters,
that it matters not.
that it matters.

remembering to hold her
in the morning,
where I hold her
as if she was everything in the world.

January 30, 2008
Brooklyn, NY

One Eye Up, Captain

Dancing shadows of the things
We don't know a slow intoxication
A frustrating burn that does not think
Again, this will be the first time?

Cascading hope, don't let me think.
That this will be the first time -
Mighty might be somehow
Sung here unto to me now, please.

A twisted turn of the wretched cargo
Then there is nothing left.
The ocean floor makes the beautiful music.
Only when it is in sync.

October 7, 2017
Oakland, CA

SATURDAY NIGHT FLICK

Those moments on your couch can be so awkward.
Just so damn awkward.
Where the words get confused and the silence is strange.
Where I know you, or I don't,
Where the hands flutter and flash
Like butterflies before a storm
Where caresses change
The hands that play
The cards that change the hands

So elegantly you lay
So quietly you play
With my delicate tenderness
My softliness
That touchliness
The quivering beats of a steady heart;
A healthy heart
Beating to
This rigidly uncertain choreography

I do not mind
That there is a lack of definition
I do not hurt
Being passive
To the fleeting pleasantry;
The ambiguity of such holiness

And yet, when I reach to touch,
When I brush upon the subject
Like a nervous hand to canvas
or the petting of unkempt hair

or the reconciliation of cocktail
or the brushing of lips to your others
or

Just a holding hand
Resting so silently on your chest
The quiet pulmonary poetry of our deafness
Where there should be nothing to understand...
That a moment is implicitly unique...
That this moment
Like the others
Are the only moments in which I exist
In your world.
The moment is always
The only time.

Our world so brief
Like that time on your couch
Where the words meant nothing
You still there, meant everything
Like all these moments.

January 19, 2008
Brooklyn, NY

STETHOSCOPE

What am I gonna do?
How is this gonna work?
I have twisted the cement blocks inside my head until they shrivel
like chicken wire against the electrical fence gauntlet that I throw myself against daily.
Such Promethean heroism contravening pressure with the Zeitgeist
Or have I an even more pretentious and Dimmsdaleian approach?
Says said maybe such bunch baby red?...
Letters that I use to color the make up of my existence?...
The twisted crimson waves of that pulse upon the wakening lucidity only obfuscate the problems of my silly, simple ebb and flow; archaic mess in the muddy tide pools of the very simple on-goings of my heretofore, here to from, here to hence and so forth.... I cannot afford to waste time and yet it is all I do... It is all... I do.

Stop me, stop me oh, oh, oh, stop me. Stop me if you've heard this one before. Here's what I thought:
Like in the here and now and in the here and how the asshole upstairs will not stop stomping around like his bitch ass is better than the rest of us and me and my fucking belly aches hurt. They fucking sting and then in a drunkenness the thing upstairs pours cocktails into the septic tank and U and I lap them up and still it stinks he thinks the mess of a world where her frustrations are the whiskeys that sting my tongue and spill my soul, they are the motivations that reap the

worlds of my attention and the selfish praise that is heaped upon the waking of the populous. It is only wasted breath as is the most usual of wasted breath and is of wasted breath which is breath. To do right, upon right, doing right of some ordinary script. But still there is the mysticism there is the unknown of the wanting to know of something.

How long must this desire persist in the epic reach dare dreams of glory hog forthright fuckyouness of the gods dying and praying of what the needs of hunger are to the point that there is no concept of right.?

How far will mercy?

How far will you take mercy?

Militant questions about dying donkeys in deserts and what did you do to feed the needing monkey of a mule who wanted to know what is what was what is what was to know the was of wasing and being to the point of just an existent to satisfy that was.

And then there are bare the bottle the meanness, the things the would teach me in the needing of the night. Somehow the sounds of a key board clack and numerical innovations of something that might matter seem like they would feed the need to be needed

...And yet I am the lonely man who cannot stomach the necessary definitionalizing of necessity...

there is only is and the gone of goneness and the problems that scream in between are not my problem, NOT MY PROBLEM,

NOT MY PROBLEM.

THERE IS ONLY these realizations that peace may be beyond human comprehension - in that frustrated poverty only epitomizes our incomprehension, then love, then no, then sex, then NO, then the child, then the essence of certain beauty and all those images of important longing;

simple thoughts and pathetic regret
the mirrors of those thoughts,
to repeat the same mistake
over... and over again...
that the ship is righted,
to hate and love.

Of course, acknowledging the general mistake of the heart beat.

January 9, 2008
Brooklyn, NY

IF I HAD THE PATIENCE OF A BILLION YEARS

I'd watch the mountains strong and still knowing they're fragile and insecure
I'd swim the oceans and their vast mysteries knowing they're future puddles
I'd see the sunset, tantalizing and serene knowing that even a star has growing pains
I'd look into the wild eyes of animals knowing their spirits return to the universe
I'd see the earth spray rain and wind knowing that it's just talking back
I'd stare at the moon spinning round and round knowing it will eventually spin out like a tired top

I'd stand by a man and know that the evil in his heart is just a mere rash on his soul
I'd stand by a grave until the soul escaped and the gravestone crumbled
I'd stand with statues and obelisks waiting 'til they fit neatly in my windowsill
I'd stand underneath the largest trees and water them like my very own flower garden
I'd stand next to my friends and enemies until we all reached a common goal
I'd stand with my love for ever and ever

October 31, 2013
Oakland, CA

TODAY

true sadness and disappointment
make everything taste better
just like salt
in a wound
or sprinkled on a steak
same bloody thing

August 26, 2010
Brooklyn, NY

30

This was not the anticipated feeling. That a distance could separate me from myself, this is not something I expected. Still, I see what I am. I look from the many angles, digital and analog, the practical, the technical. I see what I am. There is a mirror which daily acknowledges and ignores my most important strengths and weakest shortcomings.
I cannot ignore the clock of my own reflection. Such a reflection will not lie to you. That image is the only real token of time. A second, in the minute, counting a week, which will comprise the years... and then we ask, "Oh, where has the time gone."

This was not the anticipated feeling. That I could be aware of all the shortcomings. The theoreticals that are bantered amongst the most diligent academics. I know only what I know. But I hear the other tidbits. I hear some words from my far gone potential. An echo of a time that screamed an unmistakable logic to me, that is what pierces the sides of my skull this time. But they are distinct and I do hear them... yes, they sound like they are making sense.

This was not the anticipated feeling, that I would lecture anyone. I do not have that right. I do not have the experience. Yet, amidst logistical loopholes, mired in the everyday - in places where waking and sleeping are the only two alarms on both sides of the day - I do question. A constant curiosity. In contrast my friends ask me, "What did you figure out?"... or, "What did you learn?"...ultimately, "What is your point?"...

This was not the anticipated feeling. But I cannot repeat that. I cannot reiterate such precision in good conscience. To plagiarize on perfection implicates pretension. Such alliteration assumes a certain similarity. But the point... that is the point... what is the point... if there is one... and on and on. A clever cycle of never ending per plexion... ending with... some... elipses...

This was not the anticipated feeling. But the feeling stays anyway. There was a time when a certain sensation might attune personal biorhythms or ecstasies instrumentally. So this time no longer exists. This was not the anticipated feeling. That a distance could separate me from myself, this is not something I expected. The unexpected continues to be the call of the day.

This was not the anticipated feeling, me longing for a specific remedy. A prescription, an attestation, any reaction. But there is none. Maybe some conclusion makes sense, but ultimately a conclusion, only acknowledges a settlement. A settlement supposes an understanding. This is something I cannot suppose.

October 15, 2009
Brooklyn, NY

Cemetery

A crystallized headstone
massive force shattering a serenity
diminished in passing time

a stream of seconds drips
from the corners of the cross
a crawling plunge to the frozen grass

blades spinning a rotarian web
cyclically twisting a certain stasis
body and soul like earth and snow.

January 12, 2009
Brooklyn, NY

TINY CHAPTERS

I
I am folding pages from the novel of life like peels from a banana?
No. Maybe an oyster. Shucking from my thoughts the crystallized pressure of the ocean;
At least the passing of time against my weary young body.
An oyster is too hard. My soul is soft. Yes, my soul is far from anything hardened.
I understand a pearl lies beneath the rough exterior.
But I don't purport to be a shell with hidden beauties.
No, my soul might be softer - like a doughnut. I understand, there is nothing inside.
Holes - that is truly the passage of time. So many lawyers of intricate production.
Sure the ingredients are not entirely difficult. But a fried doughnut is no easy proposition.
A well crafted doughnut is, in its entirety, a collection of toppings and adornments.
A gentle hand nurtures a doughnut to its gushy interior by *topping*
The squishy hole-filled creature with a glaze of sugar and sprinkles and chocolate...
AND SOMETIMES THEY PUT IN JELLY.
Is my soul a Jelly doughnut topped with a strong dusting of confectioners' sugar?

II
I get lost looking through faces of the past.
They are not lost because they are unfamiliar to me.
They are lost because they are apart from me.

I miss my memories.
That is either obvious or redundant.
Literally memories needn't be missed.
But we all use the word memories in reflecting on times we miss.
I miss the times in which I can recall a friend.
Even if a face is apart from me, I can still recall a friend.

III
Time flows constantly, not as a reckless stream but as an overwhelming tidal wave.
The tossed ships and cracked fusion of an overwhelming show of tidal force - yes, that is Time.
Time becomes almost nothing in its immensity
The ant does not conceive of us as a person but as a vast unexplored landscape with treasures untold
We use words like traverse and explore as we conceive of temporal landscapes
Where by Time is a being unto itself and we don't even know of its individual existence.
One should not look to map this time, much as an ant will not try to understand every human finger
Which pushes it... nor heel which exterminates it.
Do not wonder when the heel or the finger will push and crush you.
A quibble with time does nothing but prevent us each from that savory moment
When friends are friends certainly in life and in forever ever
Where the mind is not bound and time does not exist.

February 24, 2015
Oakland, CA

THE FIRST SIX DAYS IN HAMILTON, NY

I

At His dawn's light we traipse upon our native ancestry.

As if some toothpaste would just clean teeth like God's shoeshine.
Raping the lock as if there were an infinite landmass to ruin.
What would the rabbit wryly say??? "that sometimes down in a gutter is the most comfortable place."
I can't help but feel lied to – I must be late to a very important date, trying to wrest myself from a bed made by one Jefferson and Confederately tucked into it by another fighting atop a round table with as penetrable chain mail of domineering confusion.
Oh, you men are all the same. Remember gentlemen, the clothes will not make you – they will only own you.
What is one able to say of a forgotten past? The muted sound of skulls and bones buried beneath our marching feet which rumble from below a cacophony of industrial fiction – the middle earth of our imperial state...
Yes Men: this is our foundation, the bangs and the whimpers.
Entitlements belong to art and to Untitled pieces from the local museums. Privilege is for those who insist on bearing witness.
The rest is uncertainty where no one owns anything but their own fear and discomfort. This never was meant to create a license to kill. That is for men from a

different time, aged special effects to distract us from our real potential. Your crystal stair remains in disrepair like your mothers have been crying about for years.

So is this where the middle passage begins? North or South of Harlem?

¡Santa Maria! Nina pintame el futuro. Seguramente que pesta. Para meterle mano hay que tener un manual... pues la real academia, se lo dejo ha España?

But why should one entertain that problem in the first place. Inquisitions that already know the answers aren't inquisitions at all – just another senseless holocaust with sails flashing to the sky like carnival weaponry.

And this poem is like any other, obnoxiously self aware and without any concrete understanding. Like the human condition, with constantly more questions *as* our answers.

But this particular moaning is not a prayer for death. ¡Here we are reclaiming!

II

The greenest earth expands from the darkest winters; coldly blown treacherousness in a land filled with the fertility of opportunity.

The winds came long ago swiftly crossing the eastern ocean, but this third planet is circular, you'll only end up where you started anyway. So to blame the swiftly crossing vessels carrying disease and torment are the same as any other.

Man forcing ways across the tides, where Cortez may have crossed the waters not looking for adventure but for a fighter... looking for a fight.

Blood cakes on our masculine hands the way mud might crust upon a weary travelers bare feet. Rain pelts the twisted metal of our fabricated earth and our meals of hardened bread from magma ovens. The cold is coming and I don't want you to be alone down there.

Rain becomes sleet, the earth hardening, tundra miles turn into the paralysis of permafrost. The stiff frigidity of the unrelenting wind swirls around the most vulnerable hearts and violently attacks the circulatory system.

The susceptibility of man to his own handcrafted demonic fantasies flourishes in his icy, icy veins. When the snowflakes descend from heavens they are cast down lightly from above, fluttering like butterflies escaping life and into death.

The icy dusting rigors man's rigid muscle so that they burst forth in stone striking fear - mothers and daughters crushed beneath the images of POWER – sons most fearful of a pummeling that would shake the faith of any god.

Oh, Man!!! This mean, nasty aggression swirls into a frigid tempest, the local population escaping as deeply into domiciles, the forever intolerance of the elements since those first few steps from the garden.

The cradle of civilization has crossed bridges of deserts bereft of water

OR bridges of this same frozen ice that forces humanity indoors.

The same dilemma exists – not whether we should escape our environments but why?

Why this fight for survival. Such a commonly held tenet of culture, that we fight and fight and fight to live.

But we do not fight to love... doesn't it beg the question?

If the snow buries the living world for ages upon ages do we maybe forget to dwell on the right questions?

When our doorsteps are rife with inert and frustrating death, the struggle for life is certainly misinterpreted

The challenge of impending doom, that death upon the land is apparently the state of our sorry human condition.

The vast expanse of monochromal idolatry intensifies man's frustration with his own self. Bound by one's own statuesque existence, breaking the shackles of stone is certainly as impossible as we imagine it. Adonis has been perfect for centuries, and Venus equally without arms - don't think such comments farce.

But to sleep and dream of a world beyond our own in the coldest hours of the darkest days we are ordained to create many myths.

Pomegranate seed fantasies give way to Doppler certainties, which insists that our realities are constantly manufactured.

Do not succumb!

Do not collapse beneath the millennial weight of pedagogical oppression!

Step on to the doorstep and dare the frostbitten tips of our hardened hearts to beat again with fresh warm blood coursing with love and compassion.

Our children cower inside convinced the snow will never melt. That the drifts and dunes that sweep across the emerald land and tuck in the brick laden industry of man may never melt. They reach for a remote control to change the channel.

Hiding in dark hovels of drunken loneliness, we think that this fight is only ours to fight alone.

¡Here we are reclaiming!

That our families are bound by ancient tradition of Household; that Brothers and Sisters are only defined by blood, the same frozen blood in our winter veins.
¡Winter IS our common experience!
From the first apple to the most recent bushel we are bound by a singular experience.
That the snow melts. ¡That is reality!... where the trees shed their leaves not because they fear the winter but because they are optimistic of the next year's foliage.
The wars of anger and cold that we perpetuate on our heart? These same hearts we have steeled against each other over time - the same boats weighed down by any millions of bound and shitting prisoners.
¡We hold ourselves captive!
This is unpasteurized history anyway - our best discoveries have always been inevitable. Penicillin lightbulbs illuminating our own self loathing is incidental, not accidental. The embrace of scientific faith is a fusion of fantasy and potential, God only knows.
¿Man fights man to the bitter end?
Nonsensical story telling of the bartered bond market trading eyes for eyes... or gods for laboratories. In an era where we deify ourselves, flying across the lands like birds, looking at instantaneous tragedy from foreign shores, we perform fantastically.
A commerce of human flesh exchanges integrity for the godlike sentences of death. ¿How long shall we brutalize this palace of potential in the name of our own anger and hate?
Beware our self-aggrandizement, do not confuse our own misunderstood evolution as an entitlement to life. The winter shuts the world in but this time to reflect

does not insist that we Spring forward to visions of control and greed.

The fall of rolling hills crusted and descending to the icy slumber of our revolutions. ¿Is that our call to action?

¿Or is our insistence to divide and conquer the divine meme?

III

Suddenly, a distant persistent feeling – one that stings of youth, like a shrinking shadow from a plane as you stare down at the dot on the ground, that singular, unique place in a universe where childhood becomes an eternity.

An emerging dot shrinks, an oxymoron, true. The tiniest shade is cast from trees swaying steadily in the same breeze from stanzas before and the same powerful forces that make us hibernate – they extend from where they were lain long ago barking logic lines confirming conformity constantly.

Angry endangered voices rough with experience and selfishness, they speak strongly. Unifiedly, they twist on sandlot slides, bear traps armed at the bottom.

The confectionary voices should attest to that want, a onceuponatime when our desires were what mattered, indulgent needs were tempered with bible neighbors studying golden rules.

The jury deliberations demand no fault and the interweb experience attacks all our modern maternal needs: ¡Our sons must breathe the freshest air! ¡¡¡Our daughters must be the loudest warriors!!!

¡Stand against the dots! ¡The canvass is ours!

¿Blank, neutral, different?... a time now for translucence. ¡¡¡Let the light shine through!!!

¿Nonsense? A lightful festival casting more color than shadow where a changing shade of magenta captivates the children for decade – ¿¿¿is that really that absurd a thought???

¡¡¡Children dancing in sunlit rainbows engulfed in a quest for self-assurance!!!... ¿¡does that phrase sting your ears?!

¡I disagree!

June 30, 2014
Boston, MA

DAUGHTER TO THE SPINNING PULSAR

That shapely hourglass, defined by luscious curves, voluptuous twists and turns from the man made measurement where definitions of seconds pour serenely, seemingly, to the bottom of our evaluation of ourselves within God's gravity,
The tiring end of the day is far more serious than a hopeful dawn when zygote eyes take in the morning light – with limitless horizon open beneath the presiding morning dreams
Dictionary visions spelled in even the best calligraphy do not imply fiction (for there is immense doubt that any of Man's records are actually even real) Soldier dreams aligned in plastic Stratego discipline, they wait for the command to march on blood-soaked mural realities:
The madmen of the mint, the hollow ghouls of classrooms, that matronly death stench from the hospital libraries - Powerpoint and printing press nightmares persist only as children nagging for attention wiping sleeves across the black and white of their festering noses.

Dawn is sacred! a riveting cacophony of orchestral motley tossing recipes of laundry spinning dizzily in a dryer of eventual chores.
Morning breaks all the dishes in the kitchen to the howl of wildlife screaming through the window, "WHAT'S FOR BREAKFAST???!!!"
As the sweat might spill from the brow to the griddle with antagonizing historical tradition and frenzied

hysteria begging at the top of its lungs... still, asking politely to those high and low for an answer.
Each day, each morning, a helix screams the question from the staple gun nooks and broken bottled crannies of a soft landing. Recesses of embedded cushioned boundaries sleeping and dreaming, rubbing eyes to a new chance for clarity.
Senseless understanding is no understanding at all - cosmic answers won't be answered merely through repetition!
Seek a cumulus cherub curiosity, the most menacing to complacent feelings, where quenching one's self on expression shall revolt against the blind, fatigued monster of tolerance.

Today is a new day, like its surrounding brethren, and like all its clones past and present - each day with its own subtle genetic defects - a beautiful misunderstanding between God and Man almost as beautiful as his children.
The mathematical sum of all days' work is miniscule next to the immeasurable hope cast from a single sip from the first drops of sunlight which spread thickly across your glistening, prism brow.
Across the crimson nectarines... to a blues for Nina growing old and wearing purple like the pristine grandmas
Bonnet doting lullabies on all the necessary tenderness the sun and stars cast on us, avenging the saddening sobriety of neglected youth.
Child, feel the crisp and eternal solar winds bringing the morning to an impassioned hopeful fusion, spreading a beacon which insists each morning is a brand new chance for shattering the hourglass and singing the perfect verse.

October 27, 2013
Oakland, CA

MAMMALS

I woke up on the wheel today-
The ride isn't so bad some days.
Sometimes, on a Monday morning
I get up and eat a piece of cheese;
Maybe I grab some crumbs in the kitchen.
I don't get too full, I save that for later
Because after I get to work
I have to worry about other things.
Sometimes I get scattered;
People ask me lots of things
At different times - I lose track.
Luckily they remember to feed me -
In the middle of the day the food is put out;
We all come to same place;
We nudge and bump each other -
As we fill plates of food and go back
Where the wheel needs spinning.
The afternoon is spent finishing
Simple wheels in need of simple spinning.
Eventually I get tired,
Everyone else gets tired of their wheels
At around the same time everyday,
Then we all get in our cars and drive home
To get up and do it again the next day.

August 7, 2017
Hanalei, HI

UN MUERTE IN EL CAJON

The box, a cage, to pack up the belongings of our history.
The relics of our past that move from each of our homes
The images and icons that are tucked beneath glass
Save them for the history books of your little box.
What if we unpack it now? To see what's been inside?
The years of anger and war mud surely line the bottom
Beneath those neatly packed memories must be the Horror
That rests beneath the cross and the rosary beads.
The pictures of the children rests on top of the Horror
Those books that they nurtured their minds must be in there
Even the fantastic ones are surely there - submarines and squids,
Dinosaurs and genetics, whales, captains and other Big Friendly Giants
including windmills and many other sweet things.
And what languages are packed into the box?
Would a box by any other name be the same?
A box? Der Karton? El Cajon? La boîte?
Who chose the words to go in there?
The ladies who moved those first boxes across,
Niña, Pinta, Santa María - such sweet names.
The language of the oppressors disguised
As seekers, in the name of crowns and jewels.
A deadly triangle persists, a death in the box,
Ein Tot in dem Karton. Un muerte in Cajon.
This is the new middle passage, here far from the original

There is no ship to box them up as cargo
No, they are already here, without a ward, without a way home
They live in this box from which there really is no escape
Beneath the ground and the water, in the skies and the magma
There is a stench of death that does not discriminate.
Each vessel of life will eventually smell.
But in this box where war and blood and imagination and truth
all battle for the respect of generations of life
The occupants forget that they are all in this together
In the box with all the words and pictures of a torrid human affair
With the earth and its many other speechless inhabitants
The scream of superiority belches forth from the cracks
The undying human need to be special and unique
And where does that get the people of Earth
Look inside that big box, mira en El Cajon
A refugee stuck in a box that does not speak his language
The refugee in a box with no name and no free currency
To trade or spend or save or give.
When the box is closed and there is no light,
only vague moments of illumination are possible upon the epochs
And our common experience teaches us nothing
Amidst the closed, dark and ruinous box.
A man beaten in his home and forced to other shores?
This is not just an old story from within the box,
No, it happens still!!! People forced to hide in the shadows,

People that run from the light - because the light is dark.
And in the darkest shadows of this box petrified colonizers still will kill
To maim, to harm, to control, to show any kind of force.
Because He is afraid.

Open the box and let the light shine on all our heirlooms
And in the corners of the box where almost all the forgotten
dust of humanity collects and covers our greatest victories
Celebrate the sun that pours around our awful
but very hard fought victories as people.
And use the past to unleash a power of empathy and compassion
So that we do not simply pack the past in to a box
But that we shine a spotlight on to all our hearts
taking brothers in arms from anywhere
they may have been lost in the box
And love them all as family and friend.
For the seas are rough across this middle passage
and under the water are the ghosts of mankind's hate
but on deck there must be room for everyone
for everyone's box of memories and contributions
to be exalted by all so that the shots we hear
are no longer gunfire from the frightened citizens of our planet
but the celebrations of achievement that humans can find
in each and every babe and parent
Because the answers are inside this box
But it must be opened to the light for all
to truly cherish all of our wonderful accomplishments.

November 15, 2016
Middletown, CA

THE WOLVES ARE OUT

The Wolves are out
The Wolves are out
The Boy is not crying tonight
A heap of shrunken lives
Upon the hilltop
Where the boy is silent

The Wolves are out
That's what they tell you
When they want you inside
But I swear they're out -
At least look out the window

The Wolves are out
I want to tell the whole world
But my crying will sound
Like silence from the dew
On the morning field after the battle

The Wolves are out
The carcasses are almost
As interesting as the rest of us
But tip toe and be concerned
They are hungry, always hungry

The Wolves are out
They can't tell a him from a whim
Snarling from hunger and cold
Snarling at anything that might taste
Good, rotting slowly down their throats

The Wolves are out and they're coming for you
They don't eat their kind
That's what one learns
If you're out on the streets
Looking across the street to a petting zoo
They're either coming for you
Or you're one of them too.

August 8, 2017
Hanalei, HI

THE ATLANTIC WAS BORN TODAY

What's the rule of law
But just a bunch of words
Where the words just matter
To the people who can afford to fight
Starving people often
Don't care to speak. No matter,
The laws were not made for them
If not to rule them.

High pine trees, knotted thorny plants, muggy tired heat
A jungle of tired plants wilting to the sidewalk next door
Dogs used to scramble beneath the shade
Foliage hanging like apples, the sun shooting high overhead
The fire and fury of the world dampened by the soft underbrush
Where shadow wallpapers the ecology.
No, not now. The cracked stone underfoot
Bikers and businessmen step through the shrubs
Chaparral, tumbleweeds, saguaros
Fractured bones of lost natural beauty are stunned
But was there anything to protect?
A moment that mattered?... so to speak.
The rule of law is penned by the privileged
Is Mother Nature subject to the rule of law?
Family fights are normal.
But don't we respect our elders?

There was a time when the words of Moses were the laws set upon the land. God was mean and his people barbaric

- warring factions of men from across the known globe - trying to avoid starvation amidst cravings. Times were hard and the bible was the law and that was how people set their calendars and solved their problems and married off their children. That was law then until it changed.

The era of nuclear proliferation politics
Science and law fused like the Enola Gay
Words have scientific weight ordained only by the faithful.
Those who are believed will always rest
Upon the tops of totems
We straddle a world that knows the debt of life
With a world that assumes life was owed to them

There are no words to fuse the souls
The fission in this medieval time is a scientific impossibility
Great bounties of energy are sacrificed
So the laws can change - arbitrary rules.
Bare bones schools where fusion isn't even in the textbooks
Skeletons reminding us of the insignificance of literacy
Surgically removed hospitals on life support
Filaments flickering in bloodless operating rooms
Churches with their bibles in the fire, congregations still cold
Entire pews filled with children running off
To the city.

Please remember this:
These buildings did not build themselves!
These corners and constructions are not accidental.
Who willed the industrialization of society?
If anything it willed me

To learn its power, to understand its language
Where the force to turn emotion into action
Is through the language of the damned.
And here we are.

So convenient the rulers can forget the laws they made
So easy the laws they made were made for them
There was a time when the laws allowed men
To package one another like an Amazon delivery
With a bulk rate just as if you were a Prime Subscriber.
Man has been waiting for drone technology for sometime.
... Oh those city nights! Light and sound awash with the benefit of privilege.
Across the middle passage men lost their lives
Man's soul overboard and the sharks victoriously feasting
At the bloody seafood buffet without a care in the world.
Nature cares not what the men high in buildings
Decide what's best for them and their children.
Yet they do it anyway - footmen of all dimensions take note
The inevitable whimpers of their masters.
Out of spite, trampling out the vintage.
Having loosed the fateful lightning of his terrible, swift sword
Never knowing really wrote His words...

...So many angry men.
They all seem so angry - and why?
Why is a person angry?
What makes the baby cry?
A mother always offers of herself first
To calm a hungry baby

So why is a person angry?
Do we change so much?
Are the needs so different?
What makes a person angry?
Feed the belly and let the mind rest...
Feed the belly again and let the mind wander
Feed the belly again and again and again...
Then might be the time to ask those questions

Mornings wind through the hills and cows are already at work
A strange land of farm hiding from suburbia.
Man tries so hard to blend in like the tall referee at midget wrestling
Such a subtlety only man can define.

August 10, 2017
Hanalei, HI

THE ALBINO MEXICAN

The bald bleached Californian and the backs of McDonald managing poverties. The names roll of the tongue - the easy ones: Jaime, David, Isaac, Jesus, Pedro, Juan, Miguel - so the list goes and the challenge increases to name the many: Rafael, Leonardo, Jorge, Fernando, Benito, Ramon, Vicente.

Moctezuma, Itzcoatl, Tizak, Cuauhtemoc, Acamapitchli - these are harder. They do not roll of the Anglo tongue. They didn't roll off the Latin tongue... and eventually the colonialism bred the new world's first mixed breed:Andrés de Tapia Motelchiuh, Pablo Xochiquentzin, Diego de San Francisco Tehuetzquititzin - something you can understand.

Names are the forgotten casualties of conquering, lost in the victory ceremonies of feasting glory or the rewarding rites to rights of rape and the bloodletting of the warrior spirit currency does not get change.

Names and names and names. They come and go attached to deadmen dreams or the infantile perfections where mothers see the eternal spirit in the eyes of their child, the untroubled babe being the closest man comes to perfection.

Then the name - naming the body, the hosting address which assumes the cloudy tempests of each and every civilization, fight and slaughtered and reduced and reintroduced with a new address, a new name for the babe.

"What's in a name, what's in a name, what's in a name," ask the refugees. Wyclef answers, "You sure you wanna hang with old Eddie Kane?" Hey Mona Lisa? No Eddie can't play the mysterious white lady. An actor is an actor is an actor... the actor is not unto themselves a fantasy. Just a name.

America Vespucci, we all stand for thee. And God, I stand for thee... how do you name justice for all? Tiffany, Jeremy, Brandon, Melissa, Annie, Alice. The blind statue of free market arguments often can't see the money that tips the scales.

What happens to the mother? Is she the unnamed deus ex machina, artificial intelligence of our souls, an anonymous source against our greedy talons and incisors.

Mothers have stumbled the streets after their mad children for years, howling for their bodies, their corpses, their restless souls, in order to name the grief and calm the rash of this planet on the skin of all the starving babies.

Convention is such a bother. The nomenclature disguises the fact that we don't care. Like one would name a sandwich or a meatball on the dinner plate only to devour her young as if they were the sandwich or some litter of meatballs.

Mothers have let these children run nameless through the streets, roughshod in the alleys, pirates of the arcade. The many children who have come to know the Legend of Zelda, or PacMan's villainous specters, the assaults on donkey kongs

Saber-rattling never felt so good. To hear the icy iron clang from the scabbard and the cold fear that lingers on the brow of the opponent. Where you look for them the next morning - yes, you now you find grave men.

Fiction has the heroes that we all adore. Romeo, and Juliet. Sara and Abraham. Han and Leia. Popocatpetl and Iztaccihuatl. Iocasta and her kid.

They have names. The same names we tell our children. All the tales we make believe. Those innocent and lewd, those tales we've told before, even in centuries of solitude. Those good days with colonel. The lover. Ursula. Becky.

The mothers have names at one point, maybe before they are bound to the agreement with nature. When the whole of a heart warms the eternity of the soul - the calm of the world rests sweetly on the songs of our mothers.

They do not need names only defense. Their patience and quietude rattles the nerves of only the rowdiest child, bullying and tussling with the other children because homework is boring and hugs are infrequent. We name those children. Give them lofty names to calm their fears. Their silence is a somehow deafening indictment. But lay blame. Do not lie blame. For an honest accounting is what the kings request.

A loneliness strikes chords against an angry harp and my eyes roll back to the top again. Pinball machines of dreaming and waking, scoring again, words colliding against that similar frame of reference - to exclaim that the play is the thing when the sentence itself is the rub.

Words landing into the wading pool of my memories or contemporaries and dreams divided and collided. Things that might satisfy a reckless mind much as the felled tree and man can sit for a while - this is no satisfaction. Time rages on like a fury men cannot understand. Women are seemingly more patient, hoping that time might heal all the wounds that man has made.

Dissatisfaction naturally sweats off the brow, and the drenching anxiety of morning attacks the bleached sides of youth. Where the colors leap and dance across from the imaginations of babes to the wailing screams of sophomoric music, the painted sides of the nursery dull after all the years when the colors must be dampened for the sale.

Mortgages that could be paid off in pickle juice and peanut butter jelly snacks for sandcastles in that lot just outside your parents window? Those are much more expensive now. Those plastic trucks and GI joes are more real now than they were then and they are actually way more expensive.

Educating the saddened mind meditating on dementia aloft above an abyss, dismal heights above the perilous depths of a mortal souls. Curious minds make for restless bedfellows, slumbering into the late mornings when the dragons whip and swirl through cocktail chandeliers and champagne fountains.

The weddings that we witness now are ornate dedications to our own fears of solitude. The loneliness screams and screams and screams like a baby, death chamber marching an all, this ode to all of those things that comfort us. The madman howling to the witnesses, "You may now kiss the bride."

Such a comeuppance for the human web of sheer dissatisfaction - constant treachery in the houses of others but in galaxies quite near to hear, a refrain comes from mysticism, "Never his mind on where he was!" The excited voice in the desolate land - the immigrant hides a scalding fear of recognition.

The negro samurais of the underground railroad do not receive the credit they deserve. You say to yourself that there were no negro samurais.... to which I say, "That is because they were so silent and effective you did not even know they were there."

African Kings, and Aztec Rulers and Chinese emperors, Black Jesus, Moor Generals, Islamic Presidents - words that sting the entrenched hypocrisy of today's kings god emperor children that monitor this life for failing pulses and limited brain activity, hoping that mindless children in prison-cell classrooms still make for deposit slip taxes.

You cannibal legislatures - we point to your dinner table served by the myths of time and the impoverished realities of the servants to your cups, overflowing with bloody fictions of meritocracy and cooperation. Blood runneth on to the floor and drowns the dark-skinned monkeys you insist swim to your table side.

What is then nonsense? Nonsense? The blanketed Fort Whimsy of my youth where the truth can find a shelf and sit like a vase while the histories of nebulae can absorb the million opportunities for myth and love to collide upon a rock like, eagles coming daily to disembowel the slumber of the great adventure.

For across the seas when the truth happens it falls to the ocean floor like the souls of those that never mattered to begin with, so they never existed in first place. Creating fictionalized realities to sort the wills of Man - in return for those many baskets of gold to the court and it's undying servitude of the rotten original sin.

And when the court is finished counting the many ends of their many rainbows and they insist the jesters come to dinner the invitees and the menu share so many of the same names: Tomas, Judas, Andrew, Diego, Samuel, Anthony, Michael, Kyle, Steve, Harrold, William... that one almost hopes they are not invited to the royal feast.

October 2, 2017
Oakland, CA

MONDAY

The computer screen
Blinking over and over
Is repetitious,

The television,
Many rainbowed images,
Drawing me closer

Like art exhibits
Pixels play upon my mind
Dancing on canvas;

Irises spring forth
Into imagination
Where spirits want rest -

Eyes are prisoners,
Witnesses of weakened men
Blinking only once.

September 8, 2017
San Ramon, CA

Agapanthus

The agapanthus blooms are wilting again, another June
here on the Central Californian shores
Up towards the crusts of the cerros and lomas tucked in
behind the water
Rivers creep through the landscape dwindling down to
inevitability and into the vast Pacific
Gravity pulls us all down to the earth eventually, for
even ashes will fall after they've risen.
The water is no different: a wave crests because it will
fall, a tide rises to retreat and the waterfall crushes the
rocks below.
Even the mountains can only fight gravity for so long, as
the water will eventually wrinkle the face like tears
tugging on an old man's skin patience will eventually
takes its toll
Time walks slowly, depending on perspectives, and
watching the hills move at an incalculably slow rate I
realize how rushed we must seem
To the flies that buzz or the scurrying mouse, time
must move like lightning - and to the gods and planets
we must look foolish and hurried.

This behavior seems normal and to a casual observer, at
the least cliche. Shameless moments are the spine of
routine and the spleen of social function;
When people take for granted their actions rather than
rehearsing the excuses for their behavior.
So we do this over and over again, bound by gravity,
rising and falling to the turning suns
When the light cascades through our windows the fight
begins, a wrestling stance positioned against the very
nature of science

Trying to move ourselves in the light against the pulling Sun and Moon, as if this were the hyperbole of ancient tales.
No, this is now, a rising fight against the morning sun to steal its energy and force this planet to meet my needs
I want this to be only my reservoir of energy flowing into and out of the fractured landscape cut by the labor of my fathers and mothers before me
A war waged against and amongst the selfish interests of my fellow man - lest I forget how typical my plight here is.
When the day is done, we cease the fight, if only because we are flawed and cannot fight the Earth forever.
We lay into the gravitational pull and rest as the Sun tugs on the warrior spirit of our fellow space travelers.

There she is in the morning, the wilted Agapanthus. Those purple leaves that stood so tall, tilt towards the earth
Parallel to the axis and askew to those leaves, dangling just above the earth and feeding from the Sun, the stalk of the agapanthus wilts.
In the blink of an eye the stalk shoots to the sky, awake and ready to fight against the cosmic bodies pulling us round in circles
The purple petals, the bulbous cocoons, that erupt in sleek geographic flowers for a saloon of other planters:
Birds, bees and the squirrels that terrorize the trees above my roof, they move about in an orbit of these earthly flowers
Then, almost selfishly, they cease to function. The stalks no longer spring above the ground, but they fall

almost ashamedly back to their genesis, as if this were not normal
But every year as the Sun stretches its light further and further out the agapanthus stalk lifts it head from its emerald pillows and goes to work
Then, like an old broken horse, the stalk limps further and further closer to its master, cracked and bent the petals long since blown away, together they weather the final storms of time,
Where eventually the spine and rigor breaks and the cells have no function but to fade.
And the gardener finally comes to sweep the debris and chase the insects and remove those useless stalks so they may be composted for next spring's soil.

August 29, 2017
Aptos CA

THOSE NEVERENDING MATH EQUATIONS

Syllables
Blocks upon more blocks
Climbing high

Sentences run long
But the imagination
Is far more complex

Paragraph labyrinth mind traps
Eviscerate their intended prey
Slurping wretched emotions.

Miracle chemistry is slaughtered
Carcasses of prose hang like participles
prepositions ending too often

Constructs should make the building safer
So why's this such a rigid way to communicate?
Are you hearing what I am trying to say?

Crying screaming tugging at wet umbilical cords
confusion incubating cocooned mother's milk creation
The war rages between the words and each person's truth

When words are scarcer what happens with feelings?
Drying like a raisin in the sun, do they defer?
Emotion should never defer to language.

Time here runs short with each utterance
The spectrum of love and hate shrinks with each word
Grammar restraining our love to give

Expanding the universe
Is as much art as it is science
Stretching minds and compassion.

The classic phrases
Will always have an impact
But we are much more.

Words will fail
Love expands depths of
Time and space.

November 30, 2017
Oakland, CA

Another Giant Wave of Sadness

There is no pretending as much as there is no hiding.
There is no protection as much as there is no happiness.
Surfing down the face of the darkness, demons twisting
In the wreaths of seaweed and the faces of fear,
In the sponge from above there is the sheer terror
That water will wipe away the sun from the earth,
Plunging into the deep deep locker below.
Dreams turn to terror like days on the water turn to nausea,
The undulation of the vast ocean of emotion swings
The pendulums of insecurity wide and far,
Bouncing across the bow, from stern to aft, when all of the sudden,
In deepening dampness of the sharp shine of the summer day,
The foggy bottom of the great below and the spun riddles of suffocation
Standing like somber wall flowers
Paralyzed underneath by the vast seas of sadness.

The waves pound against the shores where landlubbers stand.
Is there a fear that keeps them perched like sunflowers
Before their own descent beyond the Fibonacci science?
No - not here. Here there is the unscientific sequential passing
To the nether world where the sunflower seeds dry and fall
So there to does the flower itself as well. But why not plunge?!?!
Why not fall down into the dirt and the muck and the awful stench of compost.

The land buries its many fears into the worms' work.
Where the slinky centipedes and the bustling beatles climb
Over the organic carcasses without a word or worry.
The demolition of the earthly spirit is a quiet processional;
The requiems of all souls certainly find the eternal silence.
That is not for this moment - where we contemplate the slow and unemotional
Parade from big bang to big bang.
A never ending carousel upon which ride the eternal footman -
We, the yeast in their beer,
We, the ants on their meats,
We, the dirt between their toes,
That is not for one to contemplate here.
That is only the atomical bomb of nothingness.
That your own universal composition is just a brief intersection
Of electricity and good fortune.
No, not here. No, the Earth is not aware.
But the below, in the depths, where the sails and the surf
And the tide and moon and the tears and the hopeless -
They all collapse into a dark liquid obelisk that towers over
The water's surface and then, unlike any fallen tree that crushes the body,
The wave pummels the water below. The long tossing beneath the surface
Bleats the air from the lungs,
The oxygen from the capillaries,
The spirit from the heart.
There is the epitome of despondence -

A massive tube of salted water foams at the mouth
Pulling towards the rabid spirals beyond physics -
The water pulls and pulls and pulls like the baby to its own umbilical...
Where on the sea floor there are no scissors,
There is only the unending attachment to the terror.
The asphyxiating awfulness of the profoundly sad world above.
Death is that sleep, perchance to dream. And here is only the rub.
The sad unending tale of yearning - the begging for breaths and relief
Only to find the crushing emptiness of the cold ocean.

II

Pinned to the bottom of submerged canyon
One looks above to the wash and tumble of the incomprehensible world.
Sharks and dolphins spun in a mortal coil,
Twirling bodies like yins and yangs
The light skinned bellies blending in to one another.
Monochrome spirals and sparkles for a distinguished eye.
Fish which prey upon other fish which prey upon other fish
Which prey upon other fish which prey upon other fish.
No one cares, talk not of the descent,
Simple troubles for simple frenzies (no one cares).
No the crags and hollows of the cavernous ravines or the darkened palace dungeons -
There is still no escape, there is no rationale, just a darkened mystery of the pain itself.
As if questioning is not enough, there is no question that goes answered

Except for one constantly answered riddle: when will the pain return?
All the time again - all the time again.
The answer to silly questions are not so silly as they are terrifying.
How could simple confusion conjure the darkest twists of the desperate breaths?
Remember those times - when the words are breathy escapes of panic?
The unending paranoia of anxiety in the fearful breaths that come.
The simple answer would be to collapse like a sunflower,
So proud in the afternoon sun and so ashamed
Its bows its head in submission to its own brief time.
No, that is for the landlubbers, the smiling cheshire's
Dancing from myth to myth but never really attentive to the moment.
They are not submerged and caught under the sea of a rotting nothing everything.
The endless turning screw grips at the threads
Piercing further into that once unpermeated membrane.
The stinging sensation as the vessel turns
In the creeping and sweeping underwater currents,
There is just the push of just dissatisfaction.
The waves above are only the symptoms of the petrified life
Resting on the ocean floor. The exhibits of sadness within the oceanic museum
Where the world is not one's one. There is no privilege here.
There is no comfort. There is the tossing torments from above.
Tsunamis that threaten the landlubbers above.

That is no comfort and the darkened world from below is past the saddened collapse
Of the eternally giant wave. The wrecked depression of the soul
Thrust down beneath the waves where the sadness is a way of life.

November 27, 2017
Oakland, CA

THE FREEZIN' SCENE

Take forty-seven:
Skunk lying in the middle of the road
Johnny mixing the medicine
Woman descending in her old red dress
ACTION
Bags of dope dangle from the arm piercings
Tattoos fed on blood thirsty ink
Mothers crying in the streets twisting like folds of a frock
In the wind the trees twist and turn and cascading leaves
Leaving seasons turning and turning and turning and turning
The calm look of satisfaction streams across their faces
Cut! From the top!

Take forty-eight:
Deer look over the fence of a slaughterhouse
The hurricane escapes
Ships arrive in the harbor
ACTION
Starvation is one of the most familiar concepts
Children from decrepit nations and fat wealthy women tired of their own sloth
To feed a pig and to feed from a pig
The animals in the forest don't care about the corpses they consume
Since bacteria has the last laugh before life emerges
Full of maggots and penicillin

Eventually the cures to all mankind can be found in the hope of today's child...
Cut cut cut, that's not right. Try it again.

Take forty-nine:
Sewage bloats a body floating in the river
God is on the right side
The woman's child is allowed in the house
ACTION
The lights of the stadium show the lions and the Christians
Praying to a higher power has never been the same for everyone
Dungeons of greed torture the dreams of the future
Even outside amidst the burning trees and swelling tides
The doomsday device, the blindness of primates to conceive their limitations and achieve their expectations
Where the explosive nuclear power plants charge the imaginations to far off lands
That books conjure what science has disproven time and again
Yet text book functions as the check for the spirit
While the Bible promises anything one hopes to inure
Caught in the cross fire are the muddled minds and creative bellies of the less fortunate
How long will the guns keep them busy? How long can they really want to hate their neighbors?
When the sun shines and burns away the dismal distortions of kindness, the antiseptic light of our own awareness becomes a beacon of...
Cut cut cut, I hope that's not right. Take it from the top God damn it!

Take fifty:
I cooked the fish floating next to the boat
The artist has everything he needs
Put that woman in the red dress back in the attic
ACTION
Fire fire fire fire fire fire fire fire fire fire fire fire
Yeah, I went to the movies last night.
How was the show Ms. Linco...
Cut cut cut. Who wrote that cliche crap? Again!

Take fifty-one:
Modernized slaves clean our shrimp
Working with Maggie, pa and her brother
Have them hold up today's paper
ACTION
We're here talking to all the servants about man and god and law
All the good stuff the men talk about when they're thinking about
Screwing the other guys wife. Or screwing the other guy's daughter. Or just screwing the other guy.
Ain't never heard of no God actually making a law.
I heard of a lot of men making laws that God said he made.
Hearsay, is what that's called in the court of Man
But in the word of our Lord for anyone zealously representing the great Father
Hearsay is but a dream, or a man from a mount, or that man upon a cross
The world of the Lord is bandied about in the thunder and lightning of curiosities.

The images of those miracles where the water walkers and fire finders moved amongst us
Seamlessly the stories built like a bonfire built not just on faggots
But on the words of others. A contemptuous plagiarism in the form of book burnings.
That man can only stand to hear himself roar from atop the mountain.
When the echo comes back the stench of the breath of each and every respondent
Singes the eyes and burns faith to the ground.
For a faithful man has no fear
When the foul mouthed echo of his prison conjures the hate of those that are different.
No, the faithful man knows the different are just like him.
A belief that rages into the mind of righteousness and love will have no fear of those whose drummer's rim shots bounce recalcitrantly off insecure foreheads.
Cut. Again.

Take fifty-two:
Armed warriors next to ignored opium fields
I'm on the pavement.
Lobotomize the woman in the red dress please.
ACTION
I've been thinking about you so much
When are you coming home?
Soon
When?
Harry, can you come today?
Yeah... I'll come today. You just wait for me, alright?
Harry?...
I'm coming back, Marion.

Yeah.
I'm really sorry, Marion...
I know.
Cut. That's a wrap. Nice shoot everybody. Have a great weekend!

October 14, 2017
Oakland, CA

THE BRAIN OF GRAVITY

So centered in the notion of right
That it's as obvious as falling down
Truth, the slippery siren,
Screaming from the shores while the waves
Crash down, falling to the sand
Collapse one upon the other, Brother
Your sister howls in the wind.
We fight the truth like an unending war
Yet surrendering to fact day after day
As the skin falls from our faces
The dripping ruthlessness of time
Descending on our bodies
Like the darkened sky above
The sun settling in the horizon.
Shadows grow so long before our eyes
Still we insist on seeing beyond the horizon
Into the darkness
Towards a place that makes no sense
All the silly science of hundreds of years
From planet earth and into that same dark space
The fumbling understanding towards ecstasy
Like two clumsy teenagers learning for the first time
How their bodies work
The only essential aspect being the awkwardness
The right being the wrong
The facts are only opinions
This is, in fact, not a fact.
Yet arguments persist. Meaning what, I'm not sure.
Except for several observations here from this third planet:
The rain does fall. Not always noticeably nor furiously, but the rain does eventually fall.

The Earth spins tirelessly, not like an automobile tire but like a tired child.
The Sun is a giant ball of incandescent gas, it is not alone, it has many siblings.
Space is more vast than any person can imagine. Can you conceive of it all?
The attempt itself proves the rule.
When you try to fit the infinite inside anything, you will fail.
The rules that we make should not be confused with science.
There are rules, facts of the solar systems
These are more concrete than any pithy human imagination
Where the whimsy of the earthbound organism is tied to its meaty wants
The universe does not bother with whimsy,
The vacuum of space, and the squishy, hydrated nature of our own bodies...
We are no match for such a ferocious certainty.
Imagine the absolute power of always being right.
But only a real fool could think I was talking about him.
I'm sure God believes in gods... or else what point is the imagination,
The spells and incantations that our words have woven
Into the sides of cave walls,
The carved faces of canvass in museums,
Painted craterous explosions in the dirt,
Twisted metal overtures to love through song.
We are an inconsistent bunch
This motley crue of socialization we call Humankind
The rules we make are simple and amendable
We change our minds to fit our needs
Because our needs, here at this little outpost in the milky way,

Are of constant reassessment -
Human comforts forcing us to ravage through our bedrock
To evaporate the gas of millennia
To disturb our Mother one more time for warmth and security
We burn away the natural order.
As the tide is high we move on
Cars, trains, planes bustling through the absolute human need for innovation
Spewing forth our twisted view of this universe
As if this speck of pebble is the center of such a place
That the nebulae splattering the cosmos
Dare to consider our silly little lives for one moment.
Our selfishness never falls to the ground
Even these words insist that they are significant
Unless I can admit that maybe they only matter to me.
But they don't - these words explore the screen
Not because I'm interested but because I believe other people should be.
As if the rules of time and gravity apply only as I wish them to
When I wish them to
Because I wish them to.
In the end that steady invisible stream of both time and gravity
Shall beat me, like they've beaten every other person on this planet
With those truths born to my own singular experience slaughtered
Because there was no truth at all, except that I am finite,
Briefly in this moment,
While truth lingers only in that eternal battle of matter and gravity

The ultimate truth necessarily being that this is all temporary.

November 3, 2018
San Diego, CA

LEASHES

My dog gets so excited when he sees his leash
It's that thing that keeps him from being free
He'd rather be outside with the that thing on
Than inside cooped up all day long

I wonder what our leash must be
Where even just a taste of whatever it is, is so sweet
Like in love or imagination, where the thought
Is enough to occupy the mind for hours

Like gods tied to their own omnipotence
And limited by only the greatest forces
The greatest joy anything can really have
Is the one it can never quite grasp.

September 18, 2018
San Diego, CA

DOG PARK HAIKUS

Folks at the dog park
Lots and lots of barking
Sniffing each other

Concrete and fences
Where everyone roams freely
Some leashes, some laws

Odors of all sorts
Natural, artificial
Scents filling the air

The story of us
Told by the moistened entrails
In the wafting breeze

Stories are many
Told beyond human barking
By dogs at their park.

February 22, 2018
Oakland, CA

WHAT WOULD YOU BROADCAST INTO THE UNIVERSE?

What eternal question or universal truth demands a submission to the gods?
Telephone messages in so many languages. Billions of people blinking to infinity.
Lights flicker the messages of death - searing hot suns brought to their knees by physics
Waves ride across the universe on the collapsing emptiness of colliding black holes
Knowledge arrives here in the fantastic dream that we can harness the gods' expanse

What insistent claim would bring the galaxies to their knees?
Ships passing in the night silent hanging over earth like a child's mobile
Dreams careen to the wreckage of a supernatural battle
Decide which aliens deserve the right to enslave all humans.
Effort is when an individual is overmatched by their surroundings.

Can you tell the gods of time and space that you wish understood?
Understanding is the comfort food for the wayward soul.
Empathic companions will make the message travel faster.

Forgetfulness and drunkeness are the tools of understanding
Patience is the rule of the galaxy - Time always knows the story to tell.

February 12, 2018
Oakland, CA

TIGHT SPACES

Hamstring as the marathon ends
Cramps in the arms dangling in crags of caverns
Hotels in a faraway land and on currency at hand
Attics full of Christmas lights and taxidermy
Cars stuck in bumper to bumper traffic
A bathroom on any bus... really, any bus
Any cliffhanger, despite the vastness of the fall
Covers that tuck you in before story time
Lies between the one you love and the life you lead
Spoons in a hammock, 'neath some palm fronded canopy
Coffins, urns, graves and mummification
but not tombs, fires, cemeteries nor pyramids
Any moment between birth and death
The heart when it's found true love
Hands held tightly believing in one another.

April 24, 2019
Oakland, CA

HUNGER

Quiet pain inside
Growing deeper and deeper
A rumble bellows

Feeding the injured-
Instinctive evolution-
Keeps the pain away.

If there is nothing
Can you solve an empty well
With just air and hope?

Feeding the hungry...
What isn't impossible
Creates solutions.

Those empty children
Stomachs wanting nourishment
Need real food to eat.

June 20, 2019
Oakland, CA

AGAPANTHUS II

The agapanthus step out from underneath the curtain
Gardeners do not attack upon the stalk of bloom
Tentacles of summer stretching into the season
Time spinning around the bulbs
The grunge of the fungi leaves the orchids to forgive

Those damn stalks burn their blooms into the dry sun
Cells dried upon the flower, like flesh from bone.
Still like the casketed, painted like stone
Where the forever is not a matter of debate
Only a matter of interpretation

The leaves of grass sing, where the embers of spring die
The flowers of before bloom eternal
And ideas of tomorrow could never bloom.
Theorizing science is the nature of man
Whereas the nature of Nature is to consider none of this

June 26, 2019
Oakland, CA

INDEPENDENCE, OREGON

Green fields, like emeralds where the ransom for a day's peace is only a deep breath.
The trees run across the ridge like that same squirrel's tail, the one who wanted nothing to do with you.
Sunlight spackles the clouds and the hues of blue come and go in the passing shade -
From beneath such pillows, briefly escaping the bright of day - sanctuary from above;
The hills roll into the switchbacks down the mountain side, where gravity accelerates everything.

Pulling the axles and the wheels into position along the curved roads takes more concentration than it's worth.
Steering a car is a matter of survival but it can be quite restrictive.
Staying inside the lines is such an ingrained skill, you hardly notice what it might be like
If our scientific boundaries permitted us flight or excavation. We might not need such constraints
Such that we might soar over land and tunnel through the earth - alas, these are not our talents.

Nevertheless, this is some world of imagination, where the jade and amber hillsides touch upon a dream.
Here in the sanctuary of space and freedom can lines blur into a cascading wave of emotion.
For words to matter the brain must indignantly connect with this Earthly reality.
Yet among the clouds and the leaves, the spirit can soar like not like an animal but, instead, deified.

The elastic nature of the universe is always reluctant to reveal itself but when the irons are shed
One may pause and feel the freedom of one's outstretched arms, unbound, capable in any space,
When one finally arrives here in Independence after having traveled from anywhere else.

July 15, 2019
Independence, OR

ORDER

What is happening
In the ballgame they're playing
Happens all the time -

A random sequence
Bouncing between hands and toes,
Balls doing as told -

Constantly different,
Outcomes unpredictable,
Rules always the same.

August 4, 2017
Hanalei, HI

GALACTIC NOVENAS

Forced words like blood through ventricles
The power of the mind
To function without consciousness
Like the heart, like the lungs
The body transmits its many necessities without my permission
Where I dream that I may be
That existence is this intentional effort
I progress without any intention of my own
Seeking control over that which I have none.

Days alight by a sun beyond my reach
Nights descend with a darkness I cannot grasp
I react without intention
I succumb to instinct without meditation
Stars that shoot across a sky
Are no more real to me than nightmares
Wishes that beset my experience
No more actual than solar winds
Like the passage of time at the bottom of a black hole.

Answers are found less in intention than in action
The cosmic truth is far more permanent than my own
Planetary rings and bottomless wells of gravity
Far greater testaments to time and God
Where the nothingness of science is everything
My own certainty of existence a flickering fleck
Pockmarked on the skin of the earth
A particle of dust spread across a weary rock
Deep beyond my own breaths.

Where the functions of the universe

Move as motley as my own existence
The blood of physics pounds
Rules against bodies bound for brutal endings
Incalculable outcomes for which they have no concern
The irrationalities and insecurities about which I worry
Fractions of consciousness contrasted
Against the million movements within me
Over which I have no control.

July 21, 2020
Oakland, CA

A DAY OF HAIKUS

You are up early
Donating before I can
Open my own eyes.

Friends and their favors
Kind gestures, smiles, words and love
Should go hand in hand

The morning haiku
Along with some fresh coffee.
Both are uplifting!

Asleep and dreaming
My dog's having a grand time
I'm awake... less fun.

Pandemic Soccer
So quiet and tiring
Like shelter in place

Waking up at dawn
Means breakfast is so early
Is it lunchtime yet?

Faint thoughts burst to life
Vibrant sunward explosions
Feeling life in light

Moments between meals
When you are hungry for more
I'm wanting too much

Broth, both hot and cold
Varieties of liquid
Accept differences

Gasping, short of breath
Never enough oxygen
Under great pressure

Lead around by leash
I'm to lead the dog someplace...
Where are we going?

Brain decelerates
Gyrations become statutes
Movement is fantasy

Giving goes both ways
Where caring begets caring
Souls touch each other

Help is never far
Even when time and space are
When kindness prevails

Days are shortening
But with grace and sacrifice
Hope is lengthening

Dias enteros
Filled with joy; light; happiness -
Allucinante

Grateful for support

All the consideration
Made it all worth it

Goodnight sweet world
We'll try again tomorrow
I had fun today

June 22, 2020
Oakland, CA

ICE CREAM IN THE FREEZER

When grandma died there was ice cream in the freezer
There was a lot of ice cream in the freezer
Grandma had ice cream every day
Especially as the days gave way to night.
It makes sense there was so much left over
At the end of days she ate lots of ice cream
And in our hearts she will live on forever
Because of all that ice cream she left in the freezer.

February 20, 2017
Bonny Doon, CA

Also Available from Not a Pipe Publishing

BRIEF BLACK CANDLES
BY
LYDIA K. VALENTINE

"In *Brief Black Candles*, Lydia Valentine attends, with passionate velocity, to questions of survivability, remembrance and the creative art of living a fully human life, even in contexts and conditions that work against that what-it-could-be. ...reading becomes a mode of witness. ... Haptic, revolutionary and unflinching, this is a powerful debut collection by a poet who does not, and cannot, 'in this time-/ in this place-', look away."
   -Bhanu Kapil

"This debut collection, written in the most truthful key available to language, uses poetic form and precise repetition to give shape, then echo, to questions of family, loss, justice and survival, seated in the frame of an America that is a long way from post-racial—the America of today."
   -Sanam Sheriff

Wherever Fine Books Are Sold

Also Available from Not a Pipe Publishing

Strongly Worded Women
The Best of the Year of Publishing Women
An Anthology
Edited by
Sydney Culpepper

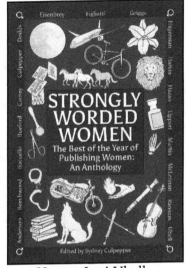

With stories by Maren Bradley Anderson, Debby Dodds, Jean Harkin, Laura Hazan, Lori Ubell, Chloe Hagerman, Lizzy Carney, Tonya Lippert, Claudine Griggs, Taylor Buccello, Julia Figliotti, Rosie Bueford, Elizabeth Beechwood, LeeAnn Elwood McLennan, Heather S. Ransom, Sydney Culpepper, and Karen Eisenbrey

Back in 2015, Not a Pipe Publishing announced accepting author Kamila Shamsie's challenge to the publishing industry to only publish women authors in 2018. After publishing eight novels by seven authors, they capped off their Year of Publishing Women with an anthology of 18 short stories by these amazing women authors from across the country.

Wherever Fine Books Are Sold

Also Available from Not a Pipe Publishing

SHOUT

An Anthology of Resistance Poetry and Short Fiction

Edited by Benjamin Gorman and Zack Dye

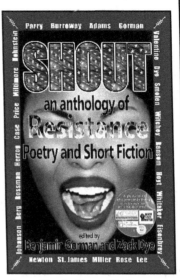

With poems and short stories by **Rosanne Parry, Janet Burroway, Carolyn Adams, Benjamin Gorman, Lydia K. Valentine, Zack Dye, Rebecca Smolen, Eric Witchey, Heather S. Ransom, Joanna Michal Hoyt, Stephen Scott Whitaker, Karen Eisenbrey, Meagan Johanson, TJ Berg, Jennifer Lee Rossman, Carlton Herzog, Austin Case, Allan T. Price, K.A. Miltimore, Jill Hohnstein, Kurt Newton, Taliyah St. James, John Miller, Christopher Mark Rose**, and **Bethany Lee.**

The 25 incredibly talented authors and poets in this anthology aren't politicians, policy wonks, or partisans. They're artists staring at the rising tide of fascism in the United States and asking you:
"What kind of world do you want to live in tomorrow?"
and "Who do you want to be today?"
And they aren't asking quietly.

Wherever Fine Books Are Sold

Also Available from Not a Pipe Publishing

by

Sang Kromah

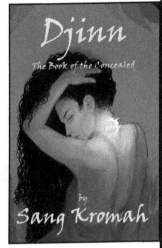

Bijou Fitzroy is strange.

As an empath, she has spent her entire life as a recluse, homeschooled by her overprotective grandmother, never allowed to stay in one place long enough to settle down and make friends. When Bijou and her grandmother move to Sykesville and she starts to attend the local high school, Bijou's world begins to crumble, town locals begin to disappear, creatures from her nightmares come to life, and she finds herself at the center of a secret war fought all around her.

"Sang Kromah weaves a tale rich in drama and TV melodrama! This is *Buffy* on acid, with all the colorful characters one would expect and more. Twists and turns - and twin heartthrobs - had me hooked from the start. A saga for the ages, and the teenagers."
  - Micayla Lally
     author of *A Work Of Art*

Wherever Fine Books Are Sold

ALSO AVAILABLE FROM NOT A PIPE PUBLISHING

Don't Read This Book
by
Benjamin Gorman

Magdalena Wallace is the greatest writer in the world. She just doesn't know it.

When she wakes up chained to a desk next to a stack of typed pages and the corpse of the person who read them, she learns just how dangerous her book can be. Rescued by a vampire, a werewolf, and a golem, she's on the run with the manuscript — and the fate of humanity — in her backpack, and a whole lot of monsters hot on her heels!

"...a whimsical, fast-paced, delight; snappily written, deliciously funny and smart, and full of affection for its characters."
- New York Times bestseller Chelsea Cain, author of *Heartsick*, *Mockingbird*, and *Gone*

"... smart, determined, and filled with really stunning prose ... maybe one of the best books I've read!"
-Sydney Culpepper
author of *Pagetown*, editor of *Strongly Worded Women*

Wherever Fine Books Are Sold